What does 'special' mean, Splodge?

I don't know – let's find out!

Pens

Helping you to get to know God more

Really Special

Written by
Alexa Tewkesbury

Every day a short Bible reading is brought to life with the help of the Pens characters. A related question and prayer apply this to daily life. Written in four sections, two focusing on the lives of Pens and two on Bible characters, young children will be inspired to learn more of God and His Word.

What's inside?

I am Special — Day 1

Where We Belong – Welcome home — Day 10

Night and Day — Day 16

Daniel's Happy Ending – Good times, bad times … God times — Day 26

Mixed Sources
Product group from well-managed forests and other controlled sources
www.fsc.org Cert no. SGS-COC-003963
© 1996 Forest Stewardship Council

'LORD … you know me. You know everything I do …'
(Psalm 139 vv 1–2)

Sharpy's **best** friend

tickle tickle tickle tickle

4

Max knows all about Sharpy.

He knows that Sharpy likes to have breakfast early. So Max has breakfast early with him. He knows that Sharpy likes to have a good run in the park. So Max has a good run in the park with him. He knows that Sharpy likes to have his tummy scratched at least once a day. So Max makes sure there's time for Sharpy's tummy-scratching every day, too.

Max knows exactly what Sharpy needs, because he knows Sharpy better than anyone.

Max is Sharpy's best friend.

 God knows us inside out and outside in.

Who do you know really well?

Pens Prayer

Thank You, Lord God, that because I am so special to You, You want to know everything about me. Amen.

Day 2

I am Special

'… from far away you understand all my thoughts.'
(Psalm 139 v 2)

Being the best

I want to be the world's best footballer!

> I can understand that. I want to be the best skateboarder.

> I want to be the world's best singer!

'I can understand that,' said Philippa. 'I want to be the best gardener.'

'I want to be the world's best hat-maker!' decided Gloria.

'I can understand that,' said Denzil. 'I want to be the best cyclist.'

Pens all wanted to be the best they could be. And because they all felt the same, they understood each other perfectly.

 God understands us perfectly because He knows us so well.

> Is there anything you would like to be 'the best' at?

Pens Prayer

Heavenly Lord, thank You that You have a special plan for my life. Teach me to trust that You only want what's best for me. Amen.

7

I am Special

'You see me, whether I am working or resting …'
(Psalm 139 v 3)

Company for Denzil

Splish, splosh, froth. Denzil filled a bucket with soapy water. His bike was muddy and needed a good wash.

Can I help?

'Lovely,' smiled Charlotte. 'I'll sing to you while you work.'

When Denzil had finished, he thought he'd have a rest.

'I'm going to watch television,' he said.

'Can I watch with you?' asked Charlotte.

'Of course,' replied Denzil. 'Keep me company … only maybe without the singing this time. If that's all right with you.'

'Lovely,' smiled Charlotte.

God loves to keep us company all day long.

You can stay and watch, if you like. Keep me company.

What do you need to do today?

Pens Prayer

Father God, it's amazing! I am so special to You that You watch over me in everything I do. Thank You. Amen.

I am Special

'Even before I speak, you already know what I will say.' (Psalm 139 v 4)

Squiggle was making a packed lunch for Splodge, and Splodge was making a packed lunch for Squiggle.

'What's in my lunch box?'

In my lunch box I'd like …

You don't need to tell me. I already know. But in *my* lunch box I'd like …

'You don't need to tell me,' interrupted Splodge. 'I already know.'

When lunch time came, they each looked in their lunch boxes.

'Wahaay!' cried Squiggle. 'You've packed exactly what I would have packed for myself.'

'Wahoo!' laughed Splodge. 'So have you!'

'Wow,' smiled Squiggle. 'That shows how well we know each other.'

 God knows everything about His special children.

Think of someone special to you. Can you guess what they'd like for lunch?

Pens Prayer

From my inside to my outside, you know me so well, dear Father. I want to spend time getting to know You, too. Amen.

I am Special

'You are all round me on every side; you protect me with your power.' (Psalm 139 v 5)

Big dog

There was a new dog in Pens' town.

It was big. Much bigger than Sharpy.

It had sharp teeth. Much sharper than Sharpy's.

It had a loud bark. Much louder than Sharpy's.

It growled. Sharpy never growled at all – and he was very frightened of it.

One day, Pens were in the park with Sharpy when …

'Woof, WOOF, **WOOF!**'

The big dog came running across the grass.

'Quick!' shouted Pens. They all huddled round Sharpy to protect him and keep him safe … and the big dog never even noticed him.

 God watches over each one of us because we are so special to Him.

Have you ever asked God to take care of you when you've been worried about something?

Pens Prayer

Father God, sometimes the things around me, or the things I have to do, may seem big and scary and difficult. Please stay close to me – to look after me and keep me safe. Amen.

Day 6

I am Special

'Your knowledge of me is … beyond my understanding.'
(Psalm 139 v 6)

Guess who?

Guess who knows what makes me really happy?

14

I do sometimes.

'But guess who knows what makes me really sad, too?' asked Marco.

'I do sometimes,' answered Gloria.

'But guess who knows everything I love and everything I hate?' continued Marco. 'Or when I'm tired and when I'm not? Or when I feel well and when I don't? Or exactly how I'm feeling ALL THE TIME?'

'Who?' puzzled Gloria.

'God!' beamed Marco. 'God knows me better than I know myself.'

 God sees everything we do and understands everything we are.

How can you get to know your friends better?

Pens Prayer

If I ever feel sad or lonely, may I remember, dear Lord, that You know me and love me completely. Amen.

I am Special

'You created every part of me; you put me together …'
(Psalm 139 v 13)

Philippa's **Picture**

Philippa had a brand-new jigsaw puzzle. The picture was of a mother swan and her baby on a twinkly blue river.

'I'm going to make that picture,' she said.

First, she opened the puzzle box and spread out all the pieces on the floor.

Next, she put together the mother swan. Then she put together the baby swan. Last of all, she put together the twinkly blue river.

'What a beautiful picture!' admired Charlotte, when it was finished.

'Isn't it?' agreed Philippa. 'And I love it all the more because I put it together myself.'

 God created everything we are – and He loves what He has made.

Have you ever made something for yourself or to give to someone else?

Pens Prayer

Lord God, thank You for putting each part of me together. Thank You that everything I am will always be so special to You. Amen.

Day 8 — I am Special

'... you saw me before I was born.' (Psalm 139 v 16)

The **special** something

What's that?

18

Something special. A daffodil.

Splodge peered inside the pot.

'It doesn't *look* like a daffodil,' she frowned. 'Daffodils are tall and yellow and pretty. That's just small and odd and a *very* funny shape.'

'That's because it's still a bulb,' Squiggle explained. 'The flower hasn't grown out of it yet.'

Squiggle and Splodge planted the bulb and, some time later, out of it grew the most beautiful daffodil.

'Wow!' cried Splodge. 'That flower's so special. We saw it before it was born!'

How special we are to God! He saw us before we were even born!

As well as bulbs, what else do flowers grow from?

Pens Prayer

Father God, You saw me before I arrived in the world and You treasure me now I am here. I really praise You. Amen.

I am Special

'… guide me in the everlasting way.' (Psalm 139 v 24)

The singing lesson

One morning, Gloria asked Charlotte, 'Could you, please, teach me to sing? I'm not very good and I'd like to be able to sing "Happy Birthday" to Philippa on her special day.'

'Of course,' Charlotte smiled. 'I'll teach you right now.'

They began by singing some 'ooohs'. They went on to sing some 'aaahs'. They tried out a few 'tra-la-las' and even several 'dum-de-dums'.

By lunch time, Gloria could sing 'Happy Birthday' perfectly.

'Thank you so much,' Gloria said. 'Philippa deserves a perfect "Happy Birthday" because she's such a good friend.'

 As God's special friends, let's show Him how important He is to us by trying to live lives that make Him happy.

Gloria wanted to sing 'Happy Birthday' to Philippa. Do you know when we celebrate Jesus' birthday?

Pens Prayer

My Father in heaven, it's amazing how special I am to You. Please teach me to love You and to share my life with You every single day. Amen.

WHERE WE BELONG

Welcome home

Day 10

'Suppose one of you has a hundred sheep and loses one of them – what do you do?' (Luke 15 v 4)

The Good Shepherd

Jesus liked to teach people about God by telling them stories. One day, He told a story about a shepherd who had one hundred sheep.

How the shepherd loved his sheep! He spent all his time caring for them. Each one had a name. Each would come to him when he called.

Then, one dreadful day when the shepherd was counting his sheep, he realised that one was missing …

 Just as each sheep was very special to the shepherd, so each one of us is very special to God.

What is made from a sheep's fluffy coat?

Pens Prayer

Thank You so much, Lord, for being my Good Shepherd and for caring for me. Amen.

Where We Belong

Welcome home

Day 11

'You leave the other ninety-nine sheep in the pasture …' (Luke 15 v 4)

Only ninety-nine

'Oh dear,' worried the shepherd. 'Oh no.'

He counted his sheep for a second time.

Then a third.

But even when he counted them for the fourth time, there were still only ninety-nine. The hundredth sheep was missing.

'Oh dear,' worried the shepherd again. 'Oh no. This is no good. I must find my missing sheep. Stay here,' he called to the others as he set off to look for her.

God doesn't want anyone to have to live without Him.

Have you ever lost something that's special to you? What did you do?

Pens Prayer

Father God, I am so small yet You love having me close to You. Thank You. Amen.

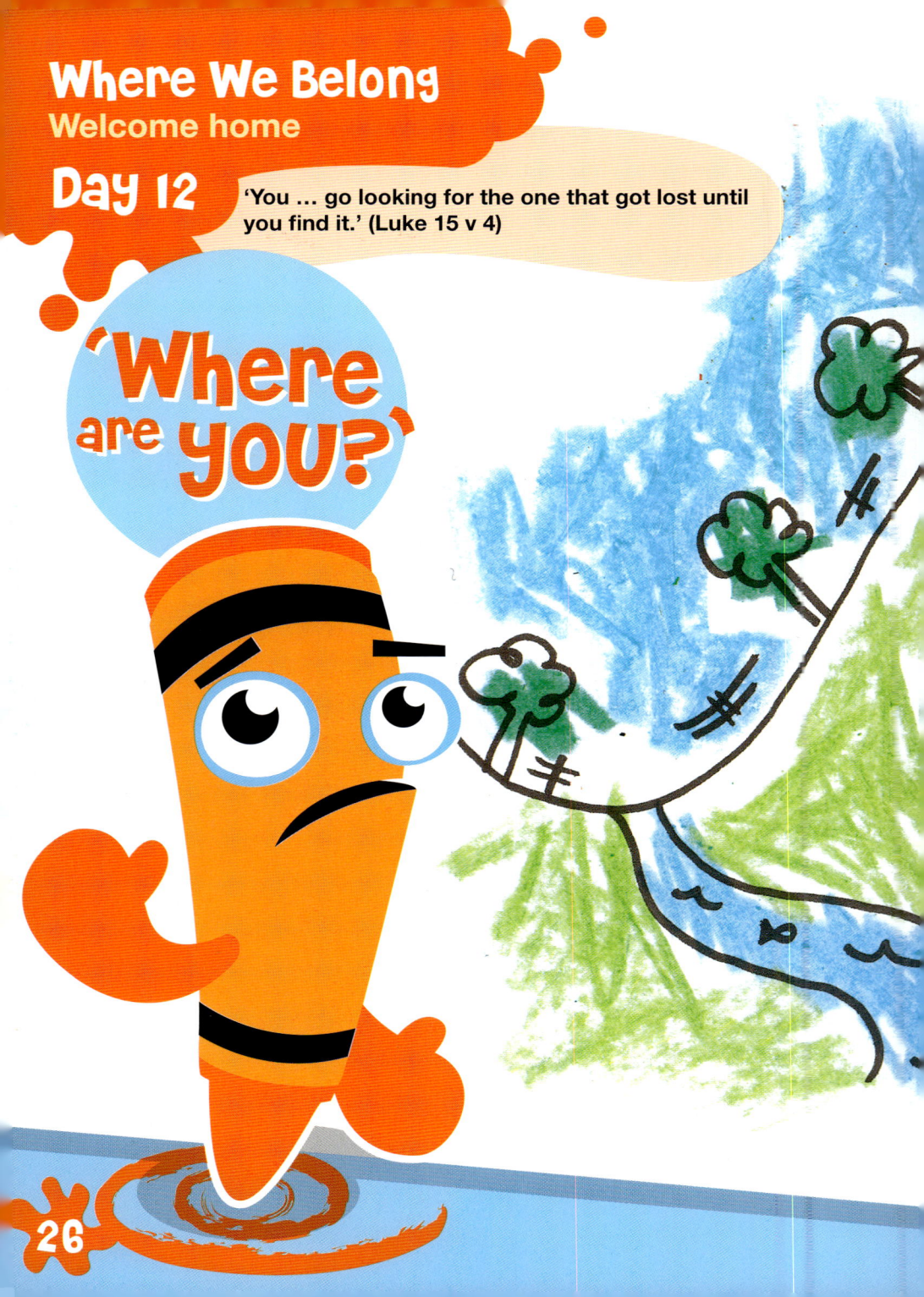

The shepherd hunted everywhere for his missing sheep.

He marched across fields.

He splashed through rivers.

He climbed up hillsides.

'Where are you?' he called.

After a while, he felt tired and he was hungry. But he wouldn't give up.

'I'm not going back,' he said, 'without my lost sheep.'

God never stops wanting us to share our lives with Him.

Who do you share your life with?

Pens Prayer

Heavenly Lord, You always love us, forgive us and care for us. You are so wonderful – thank You. Amen.

Where We Belong
Welcome home

Day 13

'When you find it, you are so happy ...'
(Luke 15 v 5)

There YOU are!

-BAAAA

The shepherd was sad. 'Supposing I never see my sheep again?' he thought.

That's when he heard it – 'Baa …'

He looked all around. There was nothing there.

'Baa … baa!' He heard it again.

The shepherd followed the sound … along a path … through some bushes … until –

'There you are!' he cried joyfully.

And there the lost sheep was! She had fallen into a hole. The shepherd lifted her carefully onto his shoulders and carried her home.

 When we call to God, He always hears us.

How can you use your voice in different ways?

Pens Prayer

Lord God, though the world is full of so many different voices, thank You that You know the sound of mine. Amen.

Day 14

'I am so happy I found my lost sheep. Let us celebrate!' (Luke 15 v 6)

Safe again

When the shepherd got home, he carried the lost sheep to where the ninety-nine others were waiting for her.

'Welcome back, little one,' he smiled.

Then, he hurried off to see all his friends and neighbours.

'Please come round to my house,' he cried. 'I have found my lost sheep. Let's have a party to celebrate that she's safely home.'

God, the Good Shepherd, loves to welcome His special children.

What makes you really happy?

Pens Prayer

Dear Father, You are always there as my very best friend. Please help me to live each day in ways that make You happy. Amen.

Where We Belong
Welcome home

Day 15

'... there will be more joy in heaven over one sinner who repents than over ninety-nine respectable people who do not need to repent.' (Luke 15 v 7)

God's welcome

Jesus finished telling His story about the lost sheep. Then He said to the people listening, 'The shepherd I have told you about is like God, and all of us are His sheep. Many people will stay close to Him. But the sheep that got lost is like someone who has done wrong things and strayed away from God.

'God never gives up hoping and waiting for that person to come back to Him.

'And when they do, He welcomes them in with open arms, because He loves them.'

No matter what happens, we will always be special to our loving Daddy God.

What could you do at the start of each brand-new day to let God know that He is special to you?

Pens Prayer

Wow, Lord God! Your love for me is brand-new with every brand-new day. How amazing – and how I praise You! Amen.

NIGHT AND DAY

'LORD God … at night I come before you. Hear my prayer …'
(Psalm 88 v 1)

Sharpy can't sleep

It was night.

A dark night.

A quiet night.

Sharpy was in his basket, but he couldn't sleep a wink. He curled up in a ball. No good. He stretched out on his side. No good. He lay on his back with his four paws in the air. It didn't make a bit of difference. He was still wide awake.

'What's wrong, Sharpy?' asked Max. 'You've been fidgeting for ages.'

Sharpy just looked sad.

'It's all right,' Max said kindly. 'It may be night, but you're not on your own. I'm here with you. Always.'

 Even in the darkest night, God is there when we need Him.

Do you know what time you go to bed at night? Do you know what time you wake up in the morning?

Pens Prayer

Father God, thank You that You are *always* with me – even in the middle of the night. Amen.

Night and Day

'... no one who waits for my help will be disappointed.'
(Isaiah 49 v 23)

Rise and shine!

ZZZZZ

It was morning.

A bright morning.

A sunny morning.

Sharpy opened one eye. So did Max.

'Yesss!' thought Sharpy. 'Night's over. Time to get up.'

'Nooo!' said Max. 'We've hardly had any sleep. It *can't* be time to get up.'

But Sharpy was ready for his breakfast. Sharpy was ready for his walk. Sharpy wasn't tired at all. He'd been awake in the night, but when he snuggled down on Max's lap, he fell asleep straight away. And just as he'd said he would, Max had stayed with him all night long.

 God's promises will last forever.

> Do you like getting up in the morning?

Pens Prayer

Heavenly Father, thank You that through the day and through the night, You'll always stay right by my side – because that's what You've promised. Amen.

Night and Day

'May the Lord himself … give you peace at all times and in every way.' (2 Thessalonians 3 v 16)

Ready to go

'Today's the day,' Charlotte bubbled happily.

'Today's the day,' Denzil sighed sadly.

Charlotte was going on holiday. She'd packed her favourite clothes to wear. She'd picked up her favourite book to read.

'What's wrong, Denzil?' asked Philippa.

'Charlotte's going away,' Denzil said gloomily. 'For three whole weeks. I'll miss her. I'll even miss her singing.'

Philippa smiled. 'Sometimes it's good to miss someone. It shows how important they are to you. But don't be sad. Your other friends are here – and we'll ask God to help you not to feel lonely.'

 God is always ready to help our friends when we pray for them.

What would you take away with you on holiday?

Pens Prayer

Thank You, Lord God, for being there when I need to talk to You about the people who are special to me. Amen.

Night and Day

'Don't be afraid … for I, the LORD your God, am with you wherever you go.' (Joshua 1 v 9)

Home again

'I'm back!' called Charlotte cheerfully.

'You're back!' yelled Denzil excitedly.

Charlotte was home from her holiday. She'd bought presents for Pens. She'd got photos to show them as well.

'Did you miss me?' asked Charlotte.

'Yes, I did,' answered Denzil. 'Did you miss *me*?'

'Yes, I did,' said Charlotte. 'Especially in the aeroplane. When I was up in the sky, you seemed a very long way away.'

'So did you,' said Denzil.

'But God was with me,' added Charlotte. 'Wherever I am, He's there.'

 There is nowhere too far away for the Lord our God.

What is the longest journey you have been on?

Pens Prayer

Dear Lord, even on the longest journey, You will be with me. What an amazing God You are! Amen.

Night and Day

'…God from whom all help comes … helps us in all our troubles …' (2 Corinthians 1 vv 3–4)

Pens had planned a trip to the funfair.

'We're going on the bumper cars!' shouted Marco and Charlotte.

'We're going on the merry-go-round!' shrieked Gloria and Denzil.

'We're going on the bouncy castle!' cried Max and Philippa. 'AND WE CAN'T WAIT!'

But when the funfair arrived in town, it rained, and Pens had to stay at home.

It rained all day … and all night. Then, the next day, the funfair moved on.

'I'm *so* disappointed,' moaned Max.

'Never mind,' said Philippa. 'Let's find some games to play indoors.'

If we ask Him, God will help us through every disappointment.

How could you comfort someone who is disappointed?

Pens Prayer

Lord God, when days don't turn out the way I want them to, may I remember that You are always ready to comfort me. Amen.

Day 21 — Night and Day

'The LORD's unfailing love and mercy still continue, Fresh as the morning, as sure as the sunrise.'
(Lamentations 3 vv 22–23)

TOP dragon

Pens were entering a painting competition. They'd painted a HUGE dragon.

Charlotte and Denzil had painted the head.

Max and Gloria had painted the body.

Philippa and Marco had painted the legs and tail.

'Our dragon is beautiful!' cried Pens. 'He's bound to win.'

They looked at all the other paintings in the competition. They were beautiful, too.

'Oh dear,' frowned Gloria. 'Supposing we don't win?'

But, guess what? Pens *did* win. They won a HUGE tin of chocolate dragons – and they all shared the prize.

 God wants to share every moment with us – the good ones as well as the bad.

Do you enjoy painting? What pictures have you painted?

Pens Prayer

Father God, I know I can talk to You when things go wrong. May I also remember to thank You when things go right. Amen.

45

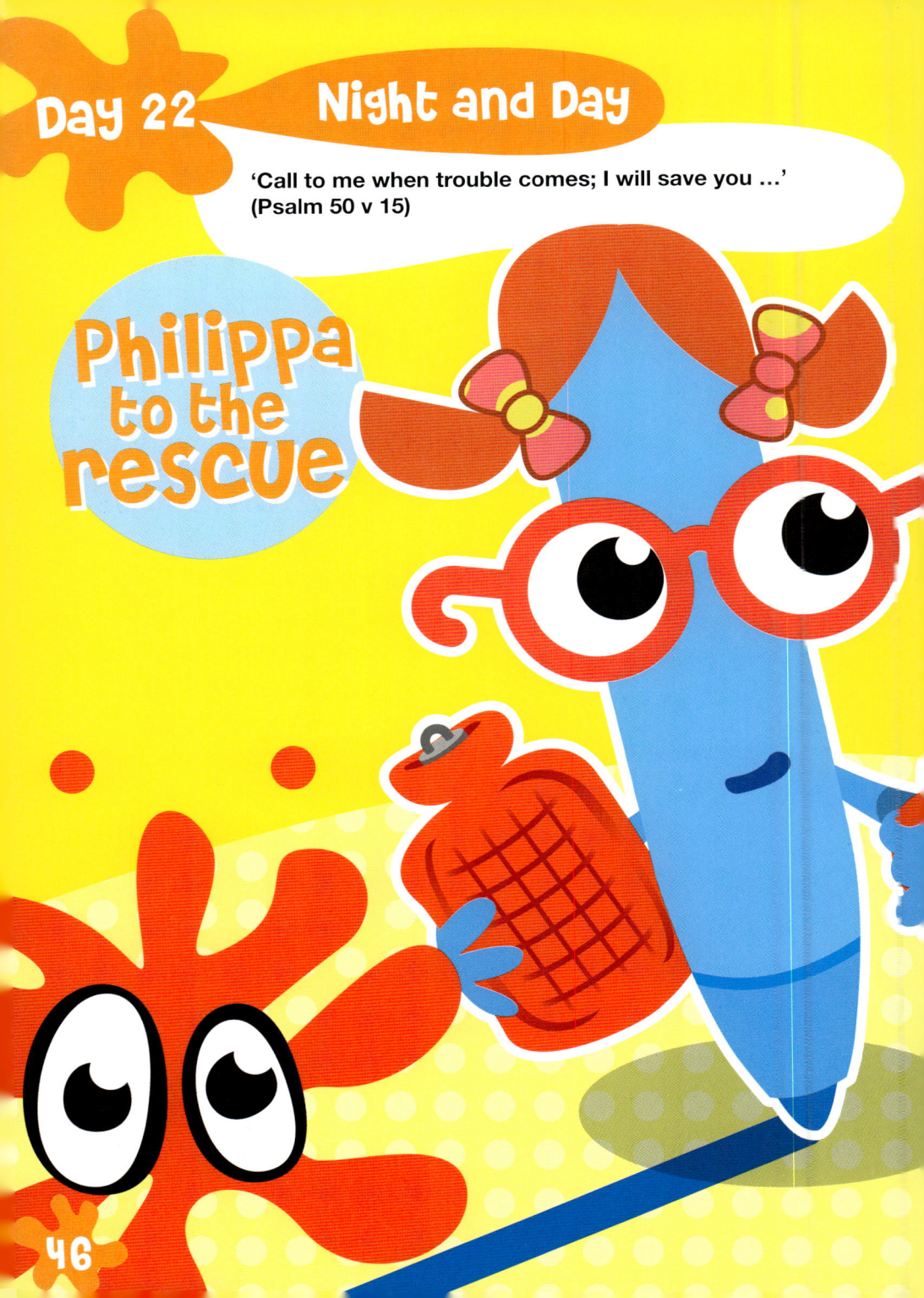

Splodge was crying.

'Whatever's the matter?' Philippa asked. 'What's happened?'

'It's Squiggle,' sniffed Splodge. 'She's not well and I don't know how to help her feel better.'

'Perhaps there's something *I* can do,' smiled Philippa.

Squiggle was in bed. Philippa tidied her covers and plumped up her pillow. She filled her a cosy hot water bottle and made her some tasty, hot soup.

'Thank you so much,' said Squiggle and Splodge.

'You're always welcome,' replied Philippa. 'Next time you need anything, please just ask. I'm always happy to help.'

 God loves us to turn to Him when we need help.

What makes you feel better when you're not well?

Pens Prayer

Thank You, Lord, that You don't just listen to me now and again – You listen to EVERY word I say. Amen.

Night and Day

'… thank the LORD for his constant love, for the wonderful things he did …' (Psalm 107 v 15)

All better

Splodge was laughing.

'I'm ready to get up!' squealed Squiggle. She bounced out of bed.

'I'm ready for breakfast!' shrieked Squiggle. She jumped down the stairs.

'Yesterday I wasn't feeling well, but today I'm ready for ANYTHING!' squeaked Squiggle. She danced around the kitchen.

Philippa arrived. 'Good morning,' she said. 'Just popping in to say hello.'

'That's very kind of you,' said Splodge, 'but you didn't need to bother. Squiggle's completely better.'

Philippa smiled. 'I don't just care about you when you're ill. I care about you all the time,' she said. 'Both of you.'

 Any time, any day, anywhere, we can be sure of God's love.

How could you be kind and caring this week?

Pens Prayer

Dear Lord, thank You for being my faithful friend. Thank You for being my constant carer. Thank You for being my heavenly Father day by day. Amen.

'… I will be with you; your troubles will not overwhelm you.' (Isaiah 43 v 2)

A bad day

Things weren't going well for Marco.

In the morning, a wheel fell off his skateboard. In the afternoon, the bell on his bike stopped working. In the evening, he broke his favourite cup.

Everything's gone wrong. It's just not my day!

Gloria knocked on the door.

'I've got a new game,' she said. 'Shall we play it together?'

'All right,' agreed Marco.

'And I've made a chocolate cake,' Gloria added. 'Shall we eat it together?'

'*All right!*' grinned Marco.

And, thanks to Gloria, suddenly Marco's day didn't seem nearly as bad.

If a day goes badly, God is always ready to cheer us up when we talk to Him.

How could you help to make a bad day better for someone?

Pens Prayer

Thank You, Lord God, that even when I'm having a difficult day, You will never leave me on my own. Amen.

Day 25 — Night and Day

'Come near to God, and he will come near to you.'
(James 4 v 8)

A brilliant day

Things were going brilliantly for Marco.

In the morning, Pens helped him to put the wheel back on his skateboard. In the afternoon, Pens helped him fix the bell on his bike. In the evening, Pens came round with a brand-new cup, exactly like the one he had just broken.

'Everything's going brilliantly!' Marco beamed. 'This is just my kind of day.'

'We like helping you,' answered Pens. 'After all, you're always ready to help us.'

'Thank you so much,' said Marco. 'You've made everything … perfect!'

When we give time to God, He loves to give us His blessings.

What blessings has God given to you? You could thank Him for them now.

Pens Prayer

Dear Lord, thank You that You are always with me, night and day, and thank You for all the good things You do for me. Amen.

DANIEL'S HAPPY ENDING

Good times, bad times … God times

Day 26

'… Daniel was reliable and did not do anything wrong or dishonest.' (Daniel 6 v 4)

A new job for Daniel

King Darius was pleased with Daniel.

'Daniel works so hard for me,' he said. 'I want him to be my special helper.'

Some of the other men who worked for the king heard this and were angry.

'We don't want Daniel giving the orders,' they complained. 'Let's get rid of him.'

They decided to tell the king about everything Daniel was doing wrong. But their plan didn't work because the king's special helper never *did* anything wrong. They'd have to think of something else.

There were bad times ahead for Daniel.

There were men who didn't like Daniel, but God watched over him.

Being the king's helper was Daniel's job. What other jobs do people do?

Pens Prayer

Dear God, please stay beside me when times are good and when times are bad. Amen.

Daniel's Happy Ending
Good times, bad times ... God times

Day 27   '... just as he had always done, [Daniel] ... prayed to God three times a day.' (Daniel 6 v 10)

Daniel follows God

The men who didn't like Daniel knew that he loved God. So they went to the king and said, 'Your Majesty, why not make it the law for the next thirty days that no one can pray to anyone but you? If anyone breaks that law,' they added, 'they will be given to the lions for supper.'

'Oh, yes!' cried the king. 'I like it!'

But nothing was going to stop Daniel talking to God. So home he went, and he knelt down beside his window and prayed.

Daniel stayed close to God, and God stayed close to Daniel.

Do you have a special place where you like to talk to God?

Pens Prayer

Thank You, Lord God, that You will never let me go. May I never let You go, either. Amen.

Daniel's Happy Ending
Good times, bad times … God times

Day 28 '… all of them went together to the king to accuse Daniel.' (Daniel 6 v 12)

Big trouble

When the men saw Daniel talking to God, they were very pleased.

'Your Majesty,' they beamed, 'Daniel is breaking your new law. He is praying to God instead of to you. Now he must be given to the lions for their supper.'

The king was very unhappy. How could he let the lions eat his special helper? But this was his own law and he couldn't break it.

'The lions are waiting for you,' he said to Daniel sadly. 'I pray that your God will save you.'

The king saw the trouble Daniel was in and wondered if God would help him.

Do you know anyone who is sad or in trouble? Tell God about them today.

Pens Prayer

Dear Father God, when things go wrong, please help me to remember that You are always beside me. Amen.

Daniel's Happy Ending

Good times, bad times ... God times

Day 29 'So the king gave orders for Daniel to be arrested ...' (Daniel 6 v 16)

Daniel for supper

The king spoke and Daniel was thrown into the lion pit.

The lions stared at him hungrily. Daniel stared back. He knew that only God could save him now.

The king was sadder than ever. Daniel wasn't just his helper. He was his friend, too.

He went back to the palace for supper – but when he thought of the lions munching on Daniel, he couldn't eat a thing. Instead he went to bed. Even then, he didn't sleep a wink all night.

But the next day, what a surprise was waiting for him …

Daniel was alone with the lions, but God knew he was in danger.

Who are your friends? Say the name of each one and thank God for them.

Pens Prayer

If I ever feel all alone, Lord God, please wrap me up in Your love. Amen.

Daniel's Happy Ending
Good times, bad times ... God times

Day 30 'He is a living God, and he will rule for ever ... He saves and rescues ...' (Daniel 6 vv 26–27)

God, the lion-tamer!

Early next morning, the king went back to the pit.

'Daniel!' he hissed. 'Are you alive? Did God save you?'

'Oh, yes!' laughed Daniel. 'The lions couldn't hurt me because God sent an angel to close their mouths.'

The king clapped joyfully and had Daniel pulled out of the pit.

'From now on,' he said, 'everyone will worship Daniel's God – the God who takes care of everyone who loves Him.'

There were good times ahead for Daniel.

Daniel trusted God through the bad times and the good – and God never left him.

Prayers are a wonderful way to praise God. How else can you praise Him?

Pens Prayer

Thank You so much, Father God, that nothing can get in the way of Your loving care for me. Amen.

Other Pens titles

  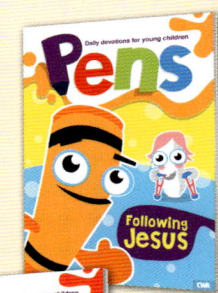

Published 2010 by CWR, Waverley Abbey House, Waverley Lane, Farnham, Surrey GU9 8EP, UK. Registered Charity No. 294387. Registered Limited Company No. 1990308.

Visit www.cwr.org.uk/distributors for list of National Distributors.

All Scripture references are from the GNB: *Good News Bible* © American Bible Society 1966, 1971, 1976, 1992. Used with permission.

Concept development, editing, design and production by CWR

Printed in China by 1010 Printing Ltd.

ISBN: 978-1-85345-569-8

OTHER CWR DAILY BIBLE-READING NOTES

Every Day with Jesus for adults
Inspiring Women Every Day for women
Lucas on Life Every Day for adults
Cover to Cover Every Day for adults
Mettle for 14- to 18-year-olds
YP's for 11- to 15-year-olds
Topz for 7- to 11-year-olds